All About Dinosaurs

Tyrannosaurus Rex

Daniel Nunn

Heinemann
LIBRARY
Chicago, Illinois

© 2015 Heinemann Library
an imprint of Capstone Global Library, LLC
Chicago, Illinois

To contact Capstone Global Library, please call 800-747-4992, or visit our web site www.capstonepub.com

All rights reserved. No part of this publication may be reproduced or transmitted in any form or by any means, electronic or mechanical, including photocopying, recording, taping, or any information storage and retrieval system, without permission in writing from the publisher.

Edited by Daniel Nunn and James Benefield
Designed by Tim Bond
Picture research by Tracy Cummins
Production by Helen McCreath
Originated by Capstone Global Library Ltd

Library of Congress Cataloging-in-Publication Data
Nunn, Daniel, author.
Tyrannosaurus rex / Daniel Nunn.
pages cm.—(All about dinosaurs)
Summary: "This book takes a very simple look at the Tyrannosaurus rex dinosaur, examining what it looked like, what it ate, how it behaved, and its special skills and features such as its enormous teeth and powerful jaws. The book also discusses how we know about Tyrannosaurus rex today, showing where fossils are found and how scientists put them together."—Provided by publisher.
Includes bibliographical references and index.
ISBN 978-1-4846-0207-2 (hb)—ISBN 978-1-4846-0214-0 (pb) 1. Tyrannosaurus rex—Juvenile literature. 2. Dinosaurs—Juvenile literature. I. Title.

QE862.S3N865 2015
567.912'9—dc23 2013040468

Acknowledgments
We would like to thank the following for permission to reproduce photographs: Getty Images pp. 9 (ROGER HARRIS), 17 (Jay P. Morgan), 18, 23 (Richard Nowitz); Science Source pp. 4 (José Antonio Peñas), 20 (Harold Brodrick); Shutterstock pp. 5a, 13 (DM7), 5b (Maria Dryfhout), 5c (Karen Givens), 5d, 23 (Piotr Gatlik), 7 bottom (Svinkin), 7 top (Sofia Santos), 8 (Elenarts), 10, 12 (TsuneoMP), 11, 14 (Bob Orsillo), 16 (MaksiMages), 19 (hans engbers); Superstock pp. 6 (NHPA), 15 (Stocktrek Images), 21 (Tips Images).

Cover photograph of Tyrannosaurus rex, reproduced with permission of Getty Images (ROGER HARRIS/SPL).

Back cover photograph of Tyrannosaurus rex reproduced with permission of Shutterstock (Elenarts).

We would like to thank Dee Reid and Nancy Harris for their invaluable help in the preparation of this book.

Every effort has been made to contact copyright holders of material reproduced in this book. Any omissions will be rectified in subsequent printings if notice is given to the publisher.

Printed in the United States 5594

Contents

Meet Tyrannosaurus Rex 4
What Was Tyrannosaurus Rex Like? .6
Where Is Tyrannosaurus Rex Now? 16
Where In the World? 22
Picture Glossary. 23
How to Say It 23
Index 24
Notes for Parents and Teachers . . .24

Meet Tyrannosaurus Rex

Tyrannosaurus rex was a dinosaur.
Dinosaurs lived long ago.

Dinosaurs were reptiles.
Snakes, crocodiles, and lizards
are reptiles that live today.

What Was Tyrannosaurus Rex Like?

Tyrannosaurus rex was a very big dinosaur.

Tyrannosaurus rex was longer than a bus!

Tyrannosaurus rex had strong back legs.

Tyrannosaurus rex was fast.

Tyrannosaurus rex had a long tail.

Tyrannosaurus rex's tail stopped it from falling over.

Tyrannosaurus rex had short arms.

Tyrannosaurus rex had very sharp teeth.

Tyrannosaurus rex had a strong bite.

Tyrannosaurus rex ate other dinosaurs.

Where Is Tyrannosaurus Rex Now?

Tyrannosaurus rex are extinct. There are no Tyrannosaurs rex alive now.

All the dinosaurs died long ago.

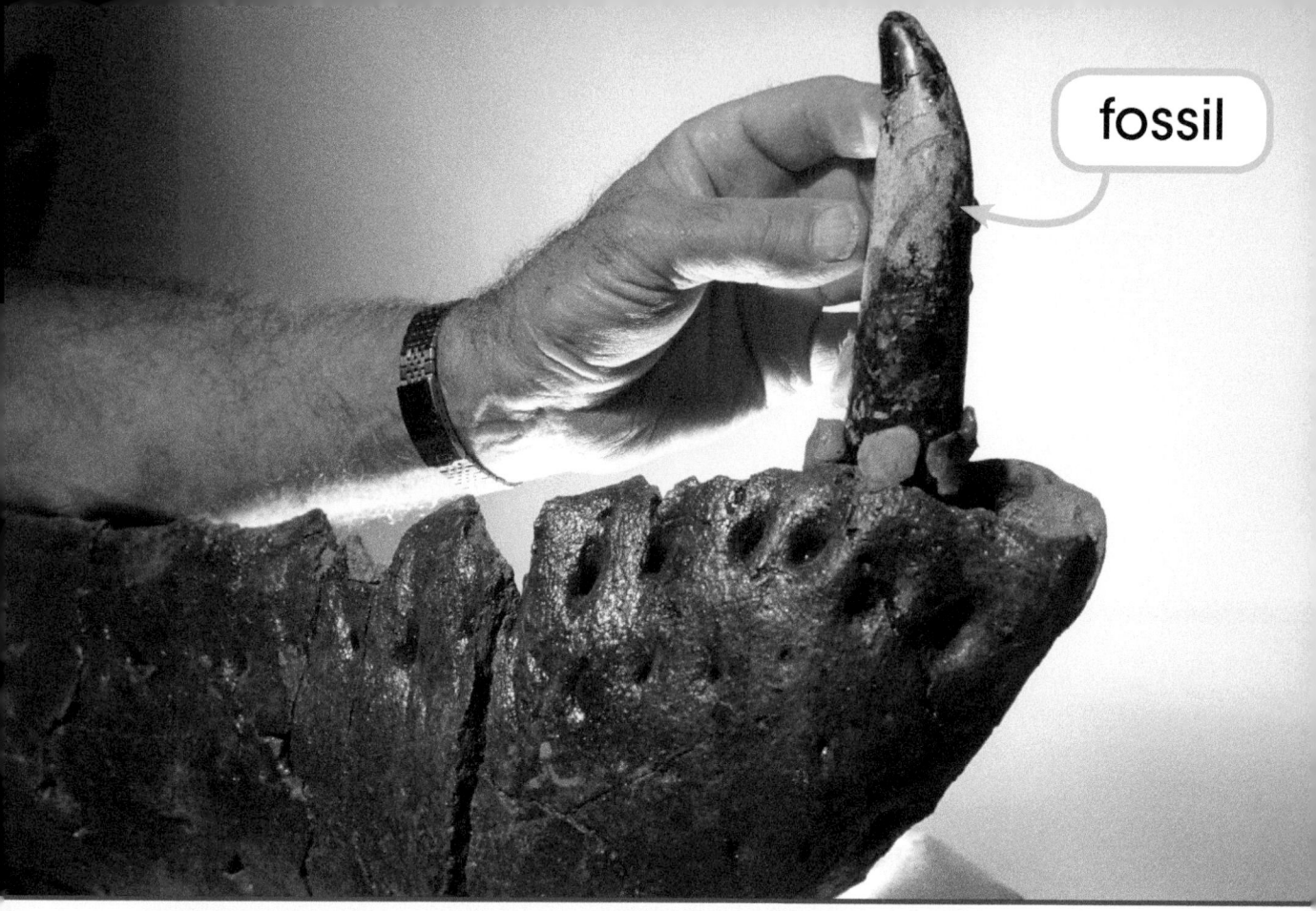

We learn about Tyrannosaurus rex from fossils.

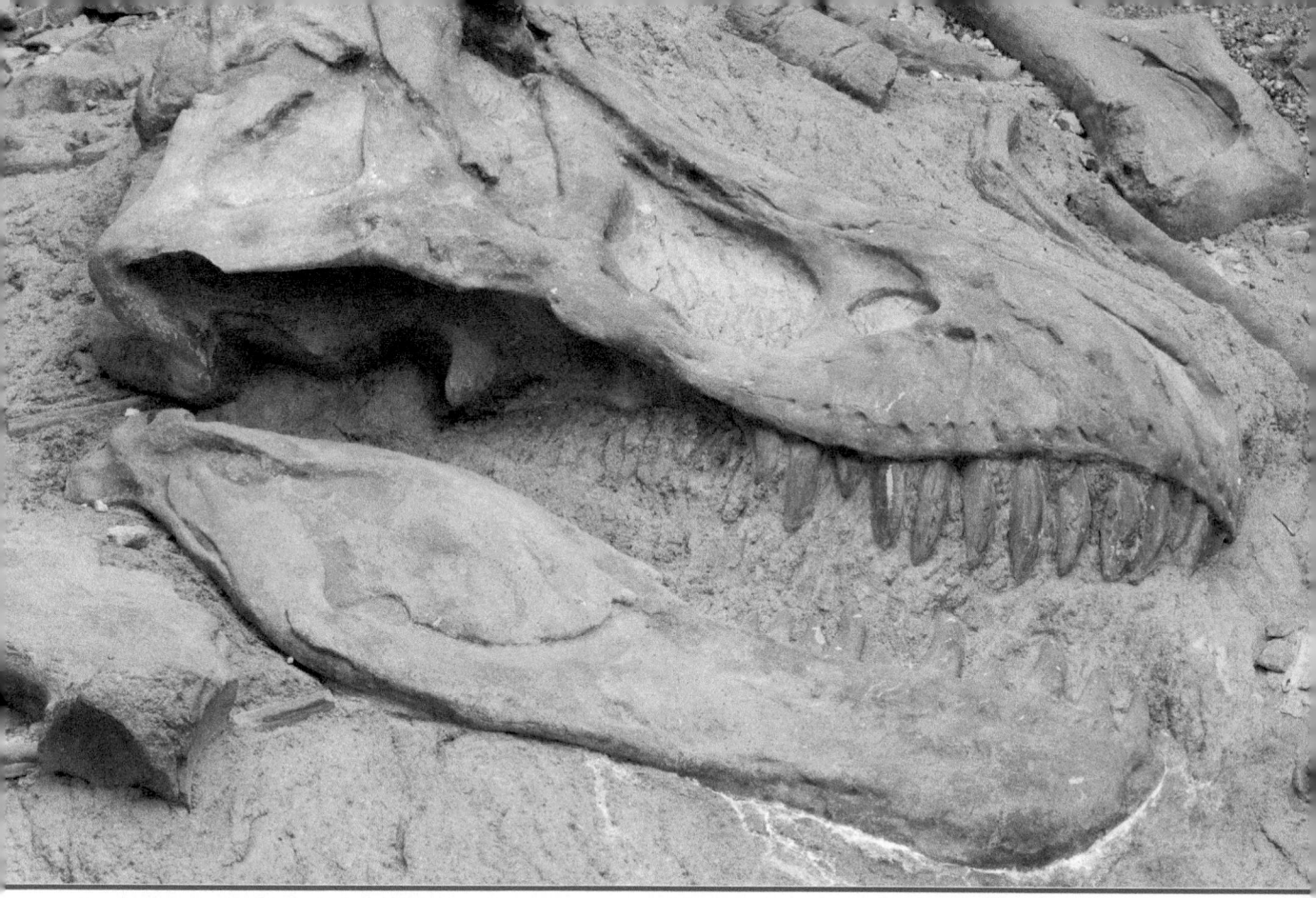

Fossils are animal bones that have turned to rock.

People find fossils in the ground.

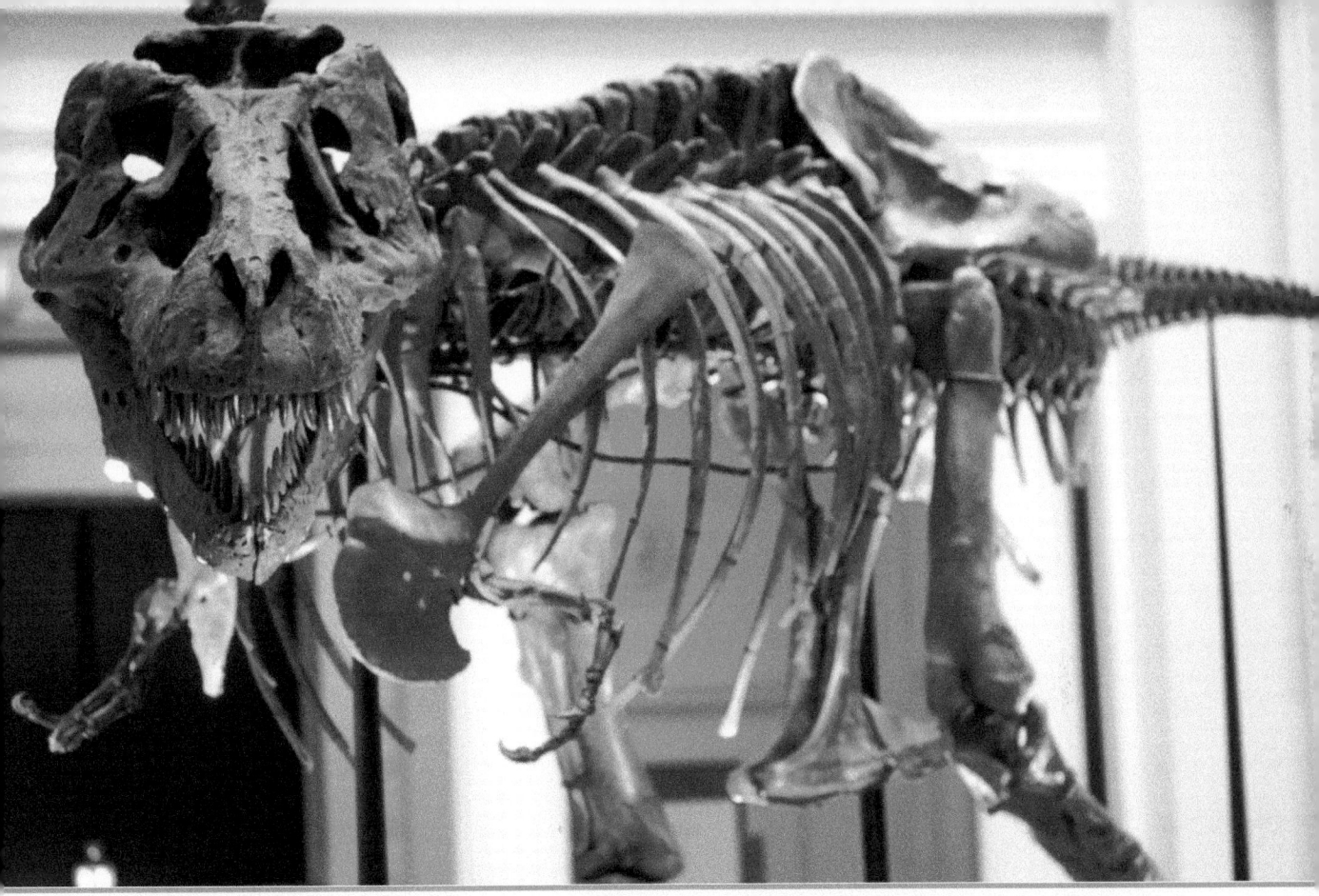

Fossils show us what Tyrannosaurus rex looked like.

Where In the World?

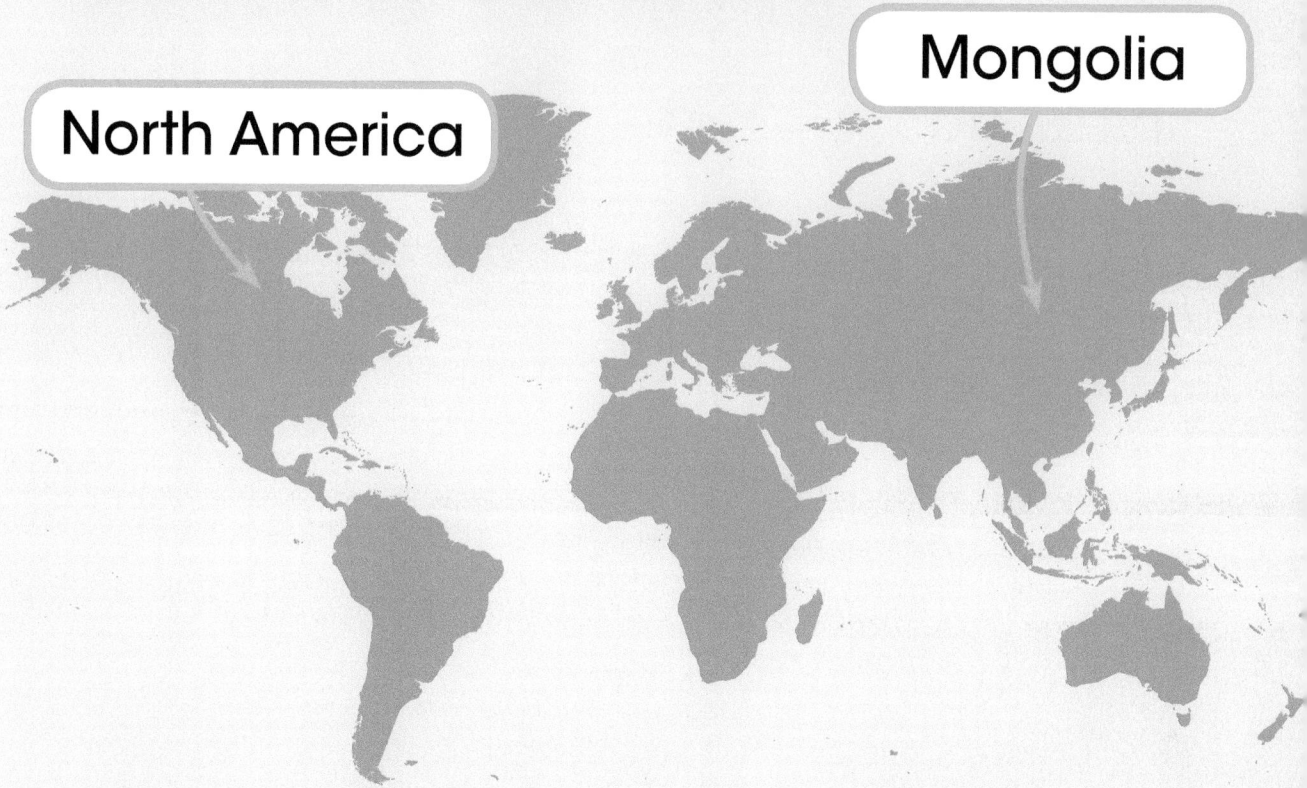

Tyrannosaurus rex fossils have been found in North America and Mongolia.

Picture Glossary

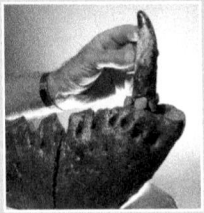

fossil animal bones or parts of a plant that have turned into rock

reptile cold-blooded animal. A lizard is a reptile.

How to Say It

Tyrannosaurus rex: say "tie-ran-uh-sawr-us rex"

Index

bite 14
crocodiles 5
fossils 18–21, 22, 23
lizards 5
reptiles 5, 23
snakes 5
tail 10–11
teeth 13

Notes for Parents and Teachers

Before Reading
Ask the children to name some dinosaurs. Ask them if dinosaurs are around today. Talk about how some dinosaurs ate plants and others ate other dinosaurs. Can they think of ways these dinosaurs might have been different? Have they heard of Tyrannosaurus rex? Find out if they already know anything about this dinosaur.

After Reading

- Make Tyrannosaurus rex sock puppets. Give each child a sock and ask the children to stick eyes on each side of the head and lots of sharp teeth in the mouth. They can add small arms at the front. Get the children to ask their puppet questions about what it was like to be a Tyrannosaurus rex.
- Make Tyrannosaurus rex teeth out of clay. They should be at least as long as a child's hand! Make sure they are sharp and then put the dry "fossils" in your own museum.